300

QUESTIONS
TO ASK
YOUR PARENTS

BEFORE IT'S
TOO LATE

300

QUESTIONS
TO ASK
YOUR PARENTS

BEFORE IT'S
TOO LATE

SHANNON ALDER

HORIZON PUBLISHERS
SPRINGVILLE, UTAH

ISBN 13: 978-0-88290-978-3

Published by Horizon Publishers, an imprint of Cedar Fort, Inc., 2373 W. 700 S., Springville, UT 84663
Distributed by Cedar Fort, Inc., www.cedarfort.com

LIBRARY OF CONGRESS CATALOGING-IN-PUBLICATION DATA

Alder, Shannon L., author.
  300 questions to ask your parents before it's too late / Shannon L. Alder.
    pages cm
  ISBN 978-0-88290-978-3 (alk. paper)
  1. Christian life--Mormon authors. 2. Life skills. 3. Parents--Death.
I. Title. II. Title: Three hundred questions to ask your parents before it's
too late.
  BV4501.3.A434 2011
  204'.4--dc22

                        2010045532

Cover design by Danie Romrell
Cover design © 2011 by Lyle Mortimer
Edited and typeset by Melissa J. Caldwell

Printed in the United States of America

10 9 8 7 6 5 4 3 2 1

Printed on acid-free paper

The unexamined life is not worth living.

SOCRATES

I dedicate this book to my dad. He has given me many great quotes like the one above. He has left me with a legacy of wisdom and I will always love him for teaching me to not walk blindly through life but to seek out the lessons others have experienced and apply what they have learned in my own life. Every person has a story to tell and we can learn from it.

And I am also thankful to my mother. You taught me that I did not need to travel far for the best lessons in life.

Jesus Christ had the best stories to tell. Without him my life would have no meaning.

CONTENTS

*He who knows all the answers has not been
asked all the questions.*

AUTHOR UNKNOWN

*We often learn great lessons in simple
and everyday ways.*

PEARL S. BUCK

INTRODUCTION

When my father suffered a heart attack and underwent a triple bypass in 2010, I flew to Arizona to be by his side. This truly insightful man taught me that wisdom was the most important thing we take with us when we depart this world. "So always seek it in life!" he would say. He pushed me to pursue a career and encouraged me to write books that will inspire others to be better. He encouraged me to read every new age book in order to gain unique perspectives on life before forming my own opinion, and to attend all kinds of workshops that would teach me enlightenment. He was and is a unique person who walked to the beat of his own drum.

As I sat there, my fragile father hooked up to several IVs in his hospital room, all I could think of was my own mortality and what legacy I would leave my children. I wondered what I would tell my children of this man who meant so much to me. He was a man of few words, but when he did speak to me, it was always in parables or stories, not unlike all the Zen, Sufi, Subud, and Buddhist books that filled the bookshelves of his den. I often felt he was more like a Shaolin priest and that I was his Grasshopper rather than his daughter. Now that old age and illness had stolen my father's remaining years, I felt some-how empty. I sat at his bedside, watching the nurses attending to him, and I felt a growing anxiety. The realization that my father was still a mystery to me was beginning to sink in. There were so many more things that I didn't know about him. And, sadly, the hour was growing too late.

With a family of my own and hundreds of miles between us, my father and I had grown to be strangers over the years. Nevertheless, I still wondered about him. What were his opinions on so many topics we had failed to discuss? How did he view his life up to this point? Had he said all he wanted to say to his children and grandchildren? What lessons had he not had a chance to teach me? At the age of forty, I still felt that pupil in me wanting direction from her life's teacher, but because of his illnesses, the communication we once had seemed to fade away.

My friends, learn from my story. Do not let those great lessons and bits of wisdom from your parents be forgotten. More often than not, old family stories and great experiences are lost forever because they are not written down. Because of this, most of us live without a sense of deep roots. We know little about our parents and what they learned in life. We all have camcorders and scrapbooks to record special occasions in our lives, but the photographs and videotapes cannot tell what we felt, how a moment changed us, or why it mattered.

One thing I have learned is that our stories are intrinsically woven together with our parents'. What they do is part of your story. What you do is part of theirs. As we move through our lives, we carry with us stories that shaped our souls. We may forget them, deny or change them, smile or suffer over them, but, like spells or charms, these stories bring back a sense of who we were and how we came to be the people we've become. In reviewing the many family history journals out there, I noticed that many asked simple questions such as "What is your favorite food?" or "What chores did you do while growing up?" These may be interesting facts to know about your parents, but they don't dig at the heart of who these people truly were—what they believed in, what their outlook on life was, and what lessons they wanted their children to learn. These are the questions I have compiled for you in this book—all the wisdom your parents have learned and want you to know.

Your children want to hear stories to reassure them that the inner strength they can muster will be sufficient against self-doubt, loss, grief, and disappointment because they know their loved ones have walked in a similar path. Your children want to know what was important to you. What lessons did you learn? How did you come to this place in your life? It doesn't matter how humble or exalted—what matters is how you got there.

Fill the pages of this book with all the thoughts you want your children to learn from you. When you're done with this book, you will hold in your hands a marvelous keepsake filled with memories, wisdom, stories, opinions, and feelings that made up every step of your life. You will be able to say, "This is all my wisdom. This is my story—my legacy to my children."

My father once said, "When I stand before God at the end of my life, I hope that I will not have a single bit of wisdom left to share and will be able to say, 'I gave all my wisdom to my children.'" Let your wisdom be your legacy that your children will remember and use as guiding light through their own lives. Namaste.

WHAT I LEARNED FROM MY YOUTH

Learning acquired in youth arrests the evil of old age; and if you understand that old age has wisdom for its food, you will so conduct yourself in youth that your old age will not lack for nourishment.

LEONARDO DA VINCI

Anybody who has survived their childhood has enough information about life to last them the rest of their days.

FLANNERY O'CONNOR

1. What is something (an event) from your childhood that has affected you the most?

_____

_____

_____

_____

_____

_____

_____

_____

2. Who were your childhood heroes?

_____

_____

_____

_____

_____

3. What was your neighborhood like growing up?

_____

_____

_____

_____

_____

4. As a child, what did you want to be when you grew up?

_____

_____

_____

_____

5. What was the most mischievous thing you did as a young-
ster?

_____

_____

_____

_____

_____

_____

_____

_____

6. How did you pull yourself out of ruts during tough times in
your childhood?

_____

_____

_____

_____

_____

_____

_____

7. How did you handle peer pressure when you were growing up?

_____

_____

_____

_____

_____

8. How has society changed since you were a youth?

_____

_____

_____

_____

_____

_____

_____

9. What are your views on alcohol and drugs? Were these things a part of your youth? How would you counsel me about using them?

_____

_____

_____

_____

10. When was a time you got in trouble for lying? What happened? What did you learn from the experience?

_____

_____

_____

_____

_____

_____

_____

_____

11. What are the greatest hardships you endured as a child?

_____

_____

_____

_____

_____

12. Have you ever taken a stand against what your friends wanted to do, or did you follow the crowd? What would you have done differently?

_____

_____

_____

_____

13. What things should I stand up for and when should I stay quiet?

_____

_____

_____

_____

_____

_____

_____

_____

14. Describe a time when you had to show courage in your youth.

_____

_____

_____

_____

_____

_____

_____

_____

_____

_____

_____

15. What do you know now that you wish you'd known when you were young?

_____

_____

_____

_____

_____

_____

_____

_____

16. How did you get through hard times with bullies at school?

_____

_____

_____

_____

_____

_____

_____

_____

17. What kind of child were you (happy, moody, popular, loner, different)?

_____

_____

_____

18. What positive or negative events in your youth affected you later as an adult?

_____

_____

_____

_____

_____

_____

_____

_____

_____

19. What did you do for fun when you were a teenager?

_____

_____

_____

_____

_____

_____

_____

_____

_____

20. Did you have any hobbies or special interests when you were a kid? How were you introduced to them?

_____

_____

_____

_____

_____

21. What were your dreams as a teenager? What did you want to do with your life?

_____

_____

_____

_____

_____

_____

_____

22. What would you teach a child about gambling? Do you believe in gambling?

_____

_____

_____

_____

_____

23. Did you ever break the law as a youth? Or come close? What did you learn from it?

_____

_____

_____

_____

_____

_____

_____

_____

_____

24. Name a time when you got in a lot of trouble with your parents and were grounded. What did you learn from that experience?

_____

_____

_____

_____

_____

_____

_____

_____

_____

25. What qualities and characteristics make a true friend?

_____

_____

_____

_____

_____

_____

_____

26. How did you go about selecting your friends in high school?

_____

_____

_____

_____

_____

27. Was there ever a time in your life when you lost your self-esteem? What did you do to rebuild it?

_____

_____

_____

_____

_____

_____

_____

28. What things bring you the most pleasure now as compared to when you were a youth?

_____

_____

_____

_____

_____

_____

29. What things frighten you now as compared to when you were a youth?

_____

_____

_____

_____

_____

30. What three things did you consider becoming when deciding on college or a career?

_____

_____

_____

_____

_____

_____

31. Are you happy with the profession you chose? Why or why not?

_____

_____

_____

_____

_____

_____

_____

_____

32. Did you go to college? If so, where, and what made you choose that school?

_____

_____

_____

_____

_____

33. What tips would you give for getting a job?

_____

_____

_____

_____

_____

34. What advice would you give about doing well in my profession?

_____

_____

_____

_____

_____

_____

35. How would you describe success in the workplace?

_____

_____

_____

_____

_____

_____

_____

_____

36. What insight can you share with me about working well with others?

_____

_____

_____

_____

37. How did you like school? What were your favorite subjects?

_____

_____

_____

_____

_____

_____

_____

38. What are your views on work ethic?

_____

_____

_____

_____

_____

39. What was your first job in high school? Did you like it? Why or why not?

_____

_____

_____

_____

_____

_____

40. What was the worst job you ever had? Why?

_____

_____

_____

41. Have you ever been fired from or quit a job? What happened?

_____

_____

_____

_____

_____

_____

42. What was the most rewarding job you ever had? Why was it rewarding?

_____

_____

_____

_____

_____

43. What awards have you received in school or at work?

_____

_____

_____

_____

_____

44. If money wasn't an object, what career would you have chosen? Why?

_____

_____

_____

_____

_____

_____

45. How do you feel about women going to college and getting a career?

_____

_____

_____

_____

_____

_____

_____

_____

46. What degrees have you earned?

_____

_____

_____

_____

47. As a youth, did you participate in Boy Scouts, Girl Scouts, or other organizations? What did you like best about them?

_____

_____

_____

_____

_____

_____

48. As a teenager, were you rebellious? If so, why? How did your parents try to guide you?

_____

_____

_____

_____

_____

_____

_____

_____

_____

_____

THE WISDOM I GAINED FROM MY FAMILY LIFE

To enjoy good health, to bring true happiness to one's family, to bring peace to all, one must first discipline and control one's own mind. If a man can control his mind, he can find the way to Enlightenment, and all wisdom and virtue will naturally come to him.

BUDDHA

1. What did you find most rewarding about being a parent?

_____

_____

_____

_____

_____

_____

_____

_____

_____

2. What advice would you give me about being a good parent?

_____

_____

_____

_____

_____

_____

_____

_____

3. What special proverbs have been passed down in your family about how to make it in life or how to have peace of mind?

_____

_____

_____

_____

_____

_____

_____

_____

_____

4. Of all the things you learned from your parents, which do you feel was the most valuable?

_____

_____

_____

_____

_____

_____

_____

_____

_____

_____

_____

5. What is your favorite memory of your parents? What were they like?

_____

_____

_____

_____

_____

_____

_____

_____

_____

_____

6. Are there any stories about famous or infamous relatives in your family? What are they?

_____

_____

_____

_____

_____

_____

_____

7. How did you and your parents learn to deal with differences?

_____

_____

_____

_____

_____

_____

_____

_____

_____

_____

8. How do you unconditionally love your children?

_____

_____

_____

_____

_____

_____

_____

_____

_____

9. How did your parents discipline you? Is that the way you would recommend I discipline my children?

_____

_____

_____

_____

_____

_____

_____

10. What makes your family truly unique compared to other families?

_____

_____

_____

_____

11. What special heirlooms—photos, bibles, or other memorabilia—have been passed down in your family?

_____

_____

_____

_____

_____

12. What was your proudest moment as a parent?

_____

_____

_____

_____

_____

_____

_____

_____

13. What is your fondest memory of your family?

_____

_____

_____

_____

_____

14. If you had it to do all over again, would you change the way you raised your family? How?

_____

_____

_____

_____

_____

15. What did you find most difficult about raising children?

_____

_____

_____

_____

_____

_____

_____

_____

16. What major illnesses or health problems affected your family?

_____

_____

_____

_____

17. Who were you especially close to in the family? Why?

_____

_____

_____

_____

_____

18. What family traditions were most important to you?

_____

_____

_____

_____

_____

_____

_____

19. Briefly tell one or more of our family's best stories or tall tales.

_____

_____

_____

_____

_____

_____

_____

_____

20. What was the best advice your parents gave you?

_____

_____

_____

_____

_____

21. What did you love most about you father? Least? Why?

_____

_____

_____

_____

_____

_____

_____

22. What did you love most about your mother? Least? Why?

_____

_____

_____

_____

_____

_____

_____

23. Why did you have the number of children that you did?

_____

_____

_____

_____

_____

24. What responsibilities did your parents require of you while growing up? How did that influence you as a parent?

_____

_____

_____

_____

_____

_____

_____

_____

_____

25. What was the easiest thing about raising a family? Why?

_____

_____

_____

_____

_____

_____

_____

26. Have you ever found yourself saying or doing things as a parent that you swore you would never say to your children? What are they?

_____

_____

_____

_____

_____

_____

_____

_____

_____

27. What differences do you see in how children are raised today compared to when you were a child?

_____

_____

_____

_____

_____

_____

_____

_____

_____

28. How did you balance your work life and your family life?

_____

_____

_____

_____

_____

_____

_____

29. What is important to you when raising children?

_____

_____

_____

_____

_____

_____

30. What do you wish you would have asked your parents?

_____

_____

_____

_____

_____

_____

31. What has having children taught you in life?

_____

_____

_____

_____

_____

_____

_____

_____

_____

_____

32. If you could write a message to your children and grand-children and put it in a time capsule for them to read twenty years from now, what would you write to them?

_____

_____

_____

_____

_____

_____

_____

_____

_____

33. What family secrets about relatives have you not told me?

_____

_____

_____

_____

_____

_____

_____

_____

34. For Mom: Did you ever have trouble during childbirth? Did you lose any children? If so, how did you get through your grief?

_____

_____

_____

_____

_____

_____

_____

_____

_____

_____

_____

35. For Dad: Were there miscarriages or troubles with child-birth? If so, how did you help Mom during this difficult time?

_____

_____

_____

_____

_____

_____

_____

_____

36. What advice would you give me for being a good sister or brother?

_____

_____

_____

_____

_____

37. Who was your favorite sibling when you were growing up? Did you ever fight?

_____

_____

_____

_____

My Views on Marriage, Relationships, and Love

Intimate relationships cannot substitute for a life plan, but to have any meaning or viability at all, a life plan must include intimate relationships.

HARRIET LERNER

We don't remember days. We remember moments.

CESARE PAVESE

1. What are your views on marriage?

_____

_____

_____

_____

_____

_____

_____

2. What advice would you give a newlywed couple?

_____

_____

_____

_____

_____

_____

_____

3. If you are married, what do you value about the relationship that you share with your spouse now?

_____

_____

_____

_____

4. What advice would you give a grandchild on his or her wedding day?

_____

_____

_____

_____

_____

_____

_____

_____

_____

5. When did you know you were in love?

_____

_____

_____

_____

6. When was your first kiss? With whom?

_____

_____

_____

_____

7. Who was your first date? What did you do?

_____

_____

_____

_____

8. What does being in love mean to you?

_____

_____

_____

_____

_____

9. What was your wedding day like?

_____

_____

_____

_____

_____

_____

_____

_____

_____

10. If you could have done anything differently on your wedding day, what would it have been?

_____

_____

_____

_____

_____

_____

_____

_____

11. How did you keep your relationships alive with your spouse while we were growing up? If you are divorced, how did you get along while raising us?

_____

_____

_____

_____

_____

_____

_____

_____

_____

_____

_____

12. What qualities and traditions make a good marriage?

_____

_____

_____

_____

_____

_____

_____

13. What have you learned about being married?

_____

_____

_____

_____

_____

_____

_____

_____

_____

_____

14. If you have been divorced, what did you learn from that experience?

_____

_____

_____

_____

_____

_____

_____

_____

_____

_____

15. During times of trouble in your life, who did you talk to about them? How did those people help you?

_____

_____

_____

_____

_____

_____

_____

16. Have you ever had a crush on or been in love with someone that didn't return your affections? How did you deal with rejection?

_____

_____

_____

_____

_____

_____

17. Have there been situations in your marriage where you gave in, in order to let your spouse be right? How did that affect the relationship?

_____

_____

_____

_____

18. Did you fight a lot with your spouse? How did you resolve your fights?

_____

_____

_____

_____

_____

19. What qualities should I look for in a mate?

_____

_____

_____

_____

_____

_____

_____

_____

_____

_____

20. What are your views on divorce?

_____

_____

_____

_____

_____

_____

_____

21. What are your views on separations?

_____

_____

_____

_____

_____

_____

_____

22. Do you believe marriage can last forever? Why or why not?

_____

_____

_____

_____

23. Describe your marriage proposal. Was your significant other surprised?

_____

_____

_____

_____

_____

_____

24. Who could you trust and depend on during your life? How did these individuals help you?

_____

_____

_____

_____

_____

25. When did you decide to marry?

_____

_____

_____

26. How do you feel about the idea of soul mates? Do you feel that there are many people out there who would have made you happy?

_____

_____

_____

_____

_____

27. What are your views on premarital sex?

_____

_____

_____

_____

28. How many times have you been engaged or come close to getting engaged?

_____

_____

_____

29. What are your views on marrying someone of another faith?

_____

_____

_____

_____

_____

_____

_____

_____

30. What are your views on marrying someone with a different cultural upbringing?

_____

_____

_____

_____

_____

_____

_____

31. How involved were your parents in your marriage? Did you ever feel they were interfering?

_____

_____

_____

_____

_____

_____

_____

_____

32. Do you believe it is okay for people to live together before getting married? Why or why not?

_____

_____

_____

_____

_____

_____

_____

_____

_____

_____

33. Have you ever been in love with someone who later broke up with you? How did you handle the situation?

_____

_____

_____

_____

_____

_____

_____

_____

34. How old were you when your parents allowed you to begin dating?

_____

_____

35. What advice would you give about how to ask someone out on a date?

_____

_____

_____

_____

_____

_____

THE PEOPLE AND THINGS THAT INFLUENCED MY LIFE

Keep away from those who try to belittle your ambitions. Small people always do that, but the really great make you believe that you too can become great.

1. What kinds of books do you like to read?

_____

_____

_____

_____

_____

_____

2. Who had the most positive influence on your life? What did that person do?

_____

_____

_____

_____

_____

3. Who helped you to develop your talents? What did they do to help you?

_____

_____

_____

_____

_____

_____

_____

4. Who is your favorite philosopher, teacher, or writer? Why is he or she your favorite?

_____

_____

_____

_____

_____

_____

_____

5. What person or book best expresses your philosophy on life?

_____

_____

_____

_____

6. What were the hardest choices you had to make in life?

_____

_____

_____

_____

_____

_____

7. Has a public speaker ever made a big impression on you? If so, who was it and what was his or her message?

_____

_____

_____

_____

_____

_____

_____

8. What principle has changed the direction of your life?

_____

_____

_____

_____

9. How do you feel about the choices you made in your life? What good choices did you make? Do you have any regrets about your choices?

_____

_____

_____

_____

_____

_____

10. What movie has most inspired you? Why?

_____

_____

_____

_____

11. What kind of music inspired or lifted you up when you felt down?

_____

_____

_____

_____

_____

_____

_____

12. If you were ever to write a book, what would it be about?

_____

_____

_____

_____

_____

_____

_____

13. What kind of friend were you to others?

_____

_____

_____

_____

_____

14. What books have you read that you enjoyed or that helped shape your life? Would you recommend that I read them?

_____

_____

_____

_____

_____

15. What television shows did you watch? Why?

_____

_____

_____

_____

_____

_____

_____

16. Where have you traveled? What are your favorite places to visit?

_____

_____

_____

_____

_____

_____

_____

17. Where in the world would you recommend I visit before I die? Why?

_____

_____

_____

_____

_____

18. Did anyone ever hurt you so much that it altered the course of your life? How did you overcome your hurt?

_____

_____

_____

_____

_____

19. What motivates you?

_____

_____

_____

_____

_____

20. What are your greatest abilities or talents? Describe a time when you used your talents.

_____

_____

_____

_____

_____

_____

_____

21. What is the most fun and interesting thing you have done in your life that you feel I should experience?

_____

_____

_____

_____

_____

22. How are you creative? What kind of things do you make?

_____

_____

_____

_____

_____

_____

23. What good deeds have you done?

_____

_____

_____

_____

_____

_____

_____

_____

24. How have you handled people that have wronged you in life?

_____

_____

_____

_____

_____

_____

25. Have you ever met anyone famous? Who?

_____

_____

_____

_____

26. Which parent taught you the most in life? What did you learn from him or her?

_____

_____

_____

_____

_____

_____

27. What family event in your life has most affected the way you look at life? Describe how it affected you and your family.

_____

_____

_____

_____

_____

_____

_____

_____

28. If you were writing the story of your life, how would you divide it into chapters?

_____

_____

_____

_____

_____

_____

_____

_____

29. What are the most important lessons you want to pass on to your children?

_____

_____

_____

_____

_____

_____

_____

_____

_____

_____

_____

30. Do you have any regrets? What are they?

_____

_____

_____

_____

_____

_____

31. Who were your best friends? How have they shaped you?

_____

_____

_____

_____

_____

_____

_____

_____

_____

32. What conferences or workshops have influenced your life?

_____

_____

_____

_____

_____

33. Did you have any addictions? How did they influence your outlook on life?

_____

_____

_____

_____

_____

_____

34. Who would you say had more influence in your life: your significant other, your family, or your friends? Why is that?

_____

_____

_____

_____

_____

_____

_____

_____

_____

35. What are your favorite sayings or expressions?

_____

_____

_____

_____

36. Have you ever lost a loved one? What happened?

_____

_____

_____

_____

_____

_____

_____

_____

MY PHILOSOPHY
ABOUT THE WORLD

Do not go where the path may lead, go instead where there is no path and leave a trail.

RALPH WALDO EMERSON

The greatest discovery of my generation is that human beings can alter their lives by altering their attitudes of mind.

WILLIAM JAMES

1. What world events had the most impact on you while you were growing up? Did any of them personally affect your family?

_____

_____

_____

_____

_____

_____

_____

_____

2. How is the world today different from when you were a child?

_____

_____

_____

_____

_____

_____

_____

_____

_____

3. What would you consider the most important inventions that have been made during your lifetime?

_____

_____

_____

_____

_____

_____

_____

_____

4. What wars have been fought during your lifetime? How did you feel about them?

_____

_____

_____

_____

_____

_____

_____

_____

_____

_____

5. How did you feel about September 11, 2001? Where were you when this happened?

_____

_____

_____

_____

_____

_____

_____

_____

_____

6. How did you feel about the Gulf War? What are your opinions about it?

_____

_____

_____

_____

_____

_____

_____

_____

_____

7. What are you views on voting? Have you ever held an office?

_____

_____

_____

_____

_____

_____

8. Who is your favorite US president? How do you feel about the office of the US president?

_____

_____

_____

_____

_____

9. Have you ever witnessed any extraordinary events? What were they?

_____

_____

_____

_____

_____

_____

10. What natural disasters—hurricanes tornadoes, floods, hurricanes, and so on—have you survived?

_____

_____

_____

_____

_____

11. How did the civil rights movement or the women's liberation movement affect your family?

_____

_____

_____

_____

_____

12. How has war affected you and your family? Which war affected you most: WWII, the Korean War, Vietnam, or the Gulf War?

_____

_____

_____

_____

_____

_____

13. Have you been politically active during your lifetime? What political party have you voted for?

_____

_____

_____

_____

_____

14. Which presidents have you voted for?

_____

_____

_____

_____

_____

_____

15. What events or trends in the media have you disliked the most? Why?

_____

_____

_____

_____

_____

_____

16. How do you feel about racial and religious prejudice?

_____

_____

_____

_____

_____

_____

17. Have you ever dedicated yourself to a cause? Which one(s)?

_____

_____

_____

_____

_____

_____

_____

_____

_____

18. Which charities did you contribute to and why?

_____

_____

_____

_____

19. Which scientific discoveries or advances have interested you the most?

_____

_____

_____

_____

_____

_____

_____

_____

_____

20. How do you view the world today? Has it stayed the same, become more evil, or become better?

_____

_____

_____

_____

_____

_____

_____

_____

_____

21. If you could change a world event that has happened, which one would it be and why?

_____

_____

_____

_____

_____

_____

_____

_____

22. Were you involved in your community? What community projects have you done?

_____

_____

_____

_____

_____

23. What do you think was the most historically significant event of your lifetime? How did it affect you?

_____

_____

_____

_____

24. What do you feel are the most important problems facing our country?

_____

_____

_____

_____

_____

_____

_____

_____

25. If you could reverse the discovery of something for the good of mankind, what would you pick?

_____

_____

_____

_____

_____

_____

26. If you could name the most worthy cause, compared to all others, what would it be and why?

_____

_____

_____

_____

_____

27. What is your view on abortion?

_____

_____

_____

_____

_____

_____

28. How do you feel about same-sex marriages and homo-sexuality?

_____

_____

_____

_____

_____

29. Has the economy ever impacted your parents or you personally?

_____

_____

_____

_____

_____

_____

_____

30. What clubs or groups did you belong to? Why?

_____

_____

_____

_____

_____

_____

31. What do you love about the country you live in?

_____

_____

_____

_____

_____

_____

_____

32. What do you love about the city or town you live in now?

_____

_____

_____

_____

_____

33. What or who has influenced your political views?

_____

_____

_____

_____

_____

_____

_____

_____

34. Have you ever killed anyone during war? What is your view on killing?

_____

_____

_____

_____

_____

35. What is your view on having weapons? Did you ever own a gun or weapon?

_____

_____

_____

_____

_____

36. Name three people you admire from history. Why do you admire them?

_____

_____

_____

_____

_____

_____

_____

_____

37. What have been the three biggest news events during your lifetime?

_____

_____

_____

_____

_____

38. If you won a million dollars, what would you do with the money?

_____

_____

_____

_____

39. Have you ever held an elected office in government or at a club? What was it?

_____

_____

_____

_____

_____

_____

40. What social movements—civil rights, women's rights, peace movements, environmental movements—have you participated in?

_____

_____

_____

_____

_____

_____

_____

_____

41. With what historical figure would you like to spend time if given a chance? Why?

_____

_____

_____

_____

42. How do you feel about the world's preoccupation with thinness and beauty?

_____

_____

_____

_____

_____

_____

_____

_____

43. How do you feel about what is viewed on television now compared to when you were growing up?

_____

_____

_____

_____

_____

_____

_____

_____

MY BELIEFS ABOUT SPIRITUALITY & RELIGION

Great men are they who see that the spiritual is stronger than any material force, that thoughts rule the world.

RALPH WALDO EMERSON

1. Do you have a philosophy on life? What's your best piece of advice on living?

_____

_____

_____

_____

_____

_____

_____

_____

2. What was your religion growing up? What church, if any, did you attend?

_____

_____

_____

3. What does Jesus Christ mean to you? If you are not Christian, what deity is important to you and why?

_____

_____

_____

_____

_____

_____

4. What have been the turning points in your spiritual life?

_____

_____

_____

_____

_____

_____

_____

_____

_____

_____

5. Do you believe in God. If so, how did you come to believe in Him?

_____

_____

_____

_____

_____

_____

_____

_____

_____

_____

6. What have you done to build your faith in God?

_____

_____

_____

_____

_____

_____

_____

_____

_____

_____

7. What do you feel is the purpose of life?

_____

_____

_____

_____

_____

_____

_____

_____

_____

8. What makes a good person in your eyes? What makes a bad person?

_____

_____

_____

_____

_____

_____

_____

_____

9. What do you believe happens to our souls when we die?

_____

_____

_____

_____

_____

_____

_____

_____

_____

_____

_____

10. Are you afraid of dying? What will you miss the most? What are you afraid of?

_____

_____

_____

_____

_____

11. Has your faith ever been tested? What did you do? Did it destroy or build your testimony?

_____

_____

_____

_____

_____

_____

12. When was a time that you went out of your way to help a person? What did you do?

_____

_____

_____

_____

_____

13. What is a motto that you have lived your life by?

_____

_____

_____

_____

14. Is there a scripture, poem, or saying that is most meaningful to you? If so, what is it and why?

_____

_____

_____

_____

_____

_____

15. Have you ever felt that you had a special calling or mission in life? What was it?

_____

_____

_____

_____

_____

_____

_____

16. Do you believe in ghosts and spirits? Why or why not?

_____

_____

_____

_____

_____

_____

17. Do you believe in heaven? How do you envision it?

_____

_____

_____

_____

_____

_____

_____

_____

18. Have you ever received an answer to a prayer? How did it change your life or faith?

_____

_____

_____

_____

_____

_____

19. Why do you have a testimony of your religion?

_____

_____

_____

_____

_____

_____

20. What lessons have you learned from helping others?

_____

_____

_____

_____

_____

_____

_____

21. What do you treasure most about your religion?

_____

_____

_____

_____

_____

_____

22. What three important things that you've learned from religion do you want to pass on to your children?

_____

_____

_____

_____

_____

_____

_____

_____

23. What is the difference between being alive and truly living?

_____

_____

_____

_____

_____

_____

24. If God could grant you one favor, what would it be? Why?

_____

_____

_____

_____

_____

25. Do you believe in guardian angels? Do you feel your loved ones who have passed away look over you? If so, how did you come to believe this?

_____

_____

_____

_____

_____

_____

26. If you had to name the most important thing that has happened in your spiritual life, what would it be and why?

_____

_____

_____

_____

_____

27. If you could pick the most sacred spot that you have ever seen in this world, where would it be? Why?

_____

_____

_____

_____

_____

28. If you had to make a case for the existence of God, what would you say?

_____

_____

_____

_____

_____

_____

_____

29. If you could have done one thing in life to make you more of a spiritual person, what would it have been? Why didn't you do that thing?

_____

_____

_____

_____

30. Is there anything in life that you wish you could undo?

_____

_____

_____

_____

_____

_____

31. If you could name the most spiritual person you have ever encountered in your life, who would that be and how has he or she affected you?

_____

_____

_____

_____

_____

_____

32. When have you felt the most spiritual in your life?

_____

_____

_____

_____

_____

33. With so many important things in a person's life, is spirituality an important quality for a person to work on? Why or why not?

_____

_____

_____

_____

_____

_____

_____

34. Do you believe in the law of attraction—that God brings people into your life to help you achieve your goals if you live worthily? Why or why not?

_____

_____

_____

_____

_____

35. Do you believe in Karma—what goes around comes around? Why or why not?

_____

_____

_____

_____

36. When was a time that you had to ask forgiveness of another person? What happened?

_____

_____

_____

_____

_____

_____

37. How do you feel about predestination? Do you feel we make life up as we go along?

_____

_____

_____

_____

_____

_____

38. Has someone hurt you in the past that you still carry a grudge about? What happened?

_____

_____

_____

_____

_____

_____

39. Have you ever changed religions? Why did you switch?

_____

_____

_____

_____

_____

40. Describe a time when your prayers were answered.

_____

_____

_____

_____

_____

_____

41. Was there ever a time in your life that someone went above and beyond to do something kind for you? What did they do?

_____

_____

_____

_____

_____

_____

_____

42. Do you believe in miracles? What miracles have occurred in your life?

_____

_____

_____

_____

_____

43. Has there ever been a time in your life that you were moved by the spirit to do something? What did you do?

_____

_____

_____

_____

_____

_____

_____

44. Did you say family prayers with your parents when you were growing up? Why or why not?

_____

_____

_____

_____

_____

45. Where do you go to relax and renew yourself? What things do you do to unwind?

_____

_____

_____

_____

_____

46. Have you ever had a paranormal experience? What happened?

_____

_____

_____

_____

_____

_____

_____

47. Do you believe we are not alone in the universe? Do you believe in extraterrestrial life? Why?

_____

_____

_____

_____

_____

_____

_____

_____

_____

WHAT I WANT YOU TO KNOW

The unexamined life is not worth living.

SOCRATES

To the questions of your life, you are the answer. To the problems of your life, you are the solution.

JO COUDERT

1. Do you still have goals and dreams for me? What are they? Have they changed as I have grown up?

_____

_____

_____

_____

_____

_____

_____

_____

2. If I could do only one thing really well in life, what would you want that to be?

_____

_____

_____

_____

_____

_____

3. Were there times that I disappointed you? What would you have had me do differently?

_____

_____

_____

_____

_____

4. How do you think we are alike? How do you think we are different?

_____

_____

_____

_____

_____

_____

_____

5. What part of our relationship do you wish we could have improved?

_____

_____

_____

_____

_____

_____

6. How do you want me to remember you?

_____

_____

_____

_____

7. What do you imagine your funeral to be like?

_____

_____

_____

_____

_____

_____

_____

8. What have I done that has made you proud?

_____

_____

_____

_____

_____

_____

_____

9. What is the one thing you want people to remember about you?

_____

_____

_____

_____

_____

10. What makes you most proud of your gender? What makes you not proud?

_____

_____

_____

_____

_____

_____

_____

_____

11. What is one thing you want me to be better at than you are?

_____

_____

_____

_____

_____

_____

12. If you could go back to any age and relive it, which would it be and why?

_____

_____

_____

_____

_____

13. How do you feel about growing older? What have been the best and worst things?

_____

_____

_____

_____

_____

_____

14. Do you feel I am a good father or mother to my children? How would you counsel me to be better?

_____

_____

_____

_____

_____

15. What is the most important thing you recommend I do or experience in my life that you did or did not get to do?

_____

_____

_____

_____

_____

_____

16. Is there anything you have wanted to say to me but never have? What is it?

_____

_____

_____

_____

_____

17. How important has physical appearance been to your life?

_____

_____

_____

_____

_____

18. What would you have done differently if no one had been there to judge you?

_____

_____

_____

_____

_____

_____

_____

19. If you were to write your own epitaph, what would it say?

_____

_____

_____

_____

_____

_____

20. If you could have avoided knowing about something in your life, what would it be?

_____

_____

_____

_____

_____

21. What was the happiest time of your life?

_____

_____

_____

_____

_____

_____

22. What was the saddest time of your life?

_____

_____

_____

_____

_____

_____

_____

23. How would you describe your life overall—difficult, easy, happy, sad, lucky, unlucky, satisfying, unsatisfying? Why?

_____

_____

_____

_____

_____

24. In your opinion, what matters most in this life?

_____

_____

_____

_____

_____

_____

_____

25. How did you feel when I was born?

_____

_____

_____

_____

_____

_____

_____

26. What's the most embarrassing thing that you have done or that has happened to you?

_____

_____

_____

_____

_____

_____

_____

_____

27. How much do you love me? My siblings?

_____

_____

_____

_____

28. Have you ever had something awful happen in your life that made you feel like giving up? What kept you from giving up?

_____

_____

_____

_____

_____

29. What grudges do you wish that you would have let go of earlier?

_____

_____

_____

_____

_____

_____

_____

_____

30. What is the most memorable phone call, card, or present you ever received?

_____

_____

_____

_____

31. How have you stayed the same during your life? How have you changed?

_____

_____

_____

_____

_____

_____

_____

_____

32. What is your typical day like now? How is it different than in the past? Is it better?

_____

_____

_____

_____

_____

_____

_____

_____

_____

33. How should people prepare for their senior years? Is there anything you would have done differently?

_____

_____

_____

_____

_____

34. If you live another thirty years, what will you do with your life?

_____

_____

_____

_____

35. What is your favorite part of your retirement years?

_____

_____

_____

_____

_____

_____

36. What things have given you the most pleasure or satisfaction in life?

_____

_____

_____

_____

_____

_____

_____

_____

37. How have your children made you proud?

_____

_____

_____

_____

_____

_____

38. What is the wisest decision you have made in your life?

_____

_____

_____

_____

_____

39. What was the worst decision of your life?

_____

_____

_____

_____

_____

_____

_____

40. How has your life changed since retirement?

_____

_____

_____

_____

_____

41. If you could change one thing about yourself physically, what would it be?

_____

_____

_____

_____

_____

_____

_____

42. If you could change one thing about yourself mentally, what would it be?

_____

_____

_____

_____

_____

43. If you could change one thing about yourself spiritually, what would it be?

_____

_____

_____

_____

_____

44. If you could change one thing about yourself emotionally, what would it be?

_____

_____

_____

_____

_____

Time is a powerful river of passing events; no sooner is one thing brought to sight than it is swept away and another takes its place—and this, too, will be swept away.

MARCUS AURELIUS

You don't get to choose how or when you die. You only get to choose how you're going to live.

JOAN BAEZ

About the Author

Shannon Alder is the author of *300 Questions LDS Couples Should Ask Before Marriage* and *300 Questions LDS Couples Should Ask for a More Vibrant Marriage*. She majored in physical therapy and works as an inpatient therapist at a rehabilitation hospital in California. Her father taught her early on to question everything in life and then write it all down so others could benefit from what she learned. Because of him, writing has been her passion. However, when she is not typing away at the computer or hiking with her husband, she spends the rest of her time devoted to the two most precious people in her life—her two beautiful boys, Indiana and Arizona. You can learn more about her books by visiting her author website at shannonalder.com.

When we go before Him, God will ask, "Where are your wounds?" And we will say, "I have no wounds." And God will ask, "Was there nothing worth fighting for?"

REVEREND ALLAN BOESAK